A YEAR OF SACRED CIRCLES

HEARING NATURE'S VOICE IN SILENT CONVERSATIONS

Written and Illustrated by Beth Adoette

Copyright © 2018 Beth Adoette

All rights reserved.

All rights reserved. No part of this book, text or illustrations, may be reproduced, distributed, or transmitted in any manner whatsoever without the express written permission of the publisher, except for the use of brief quotations in a book review.

First Printing, 2018
ISBN-13: 978-1985860612
ISBN-10: 1985860619
Printed in the United States of America

Published by Beth Adoette
www.bethadoette.com

Introduction

A new year doesn't necessarily start in January. It starts when you begin. This *Year of Sacred Circles* began one December as I briskly walked down the middle of a country road, anticipating the creation of some sort of circle under a favorite tree.

That experience was a milestone moment and the beginning of a journey creating what I now call "Contemplative Sacred Circles." These changing circles gently hold the physical and spiritual message of the moment; the wordless conversation between nature, the Creator, and me. In that place, in that moment, I am always surprised by the wisdom I find.

I think of a year not as twelve months, but as the completion of a circle of seasons. The twelve contemplative circles in this title document moments, rather than months. All, with the exception of "Another Moment," are shown in the order in which they were created.

I define sacred as something holy and set apart. A place of awe and wonder.

And circles, ancient symbols used by seekers of so many faiths all over the world and throughout the ages? To me, they are symbols of beauty, inclusion, and generosity.

This *Year of Sacred Circles* started in silence under a humble little oak. It ended with a gentle yet powerful invitation to challenge the way I see myself and the world in which I am placed. I invite you to join the conversation.

dedicated to the little oak that
reaches up and reaches out
where the river and the ocean meet

Here at the base of the tree, without words, we told each other we understood. Despite our hardships, we agreed to continue to reach up and reach out.

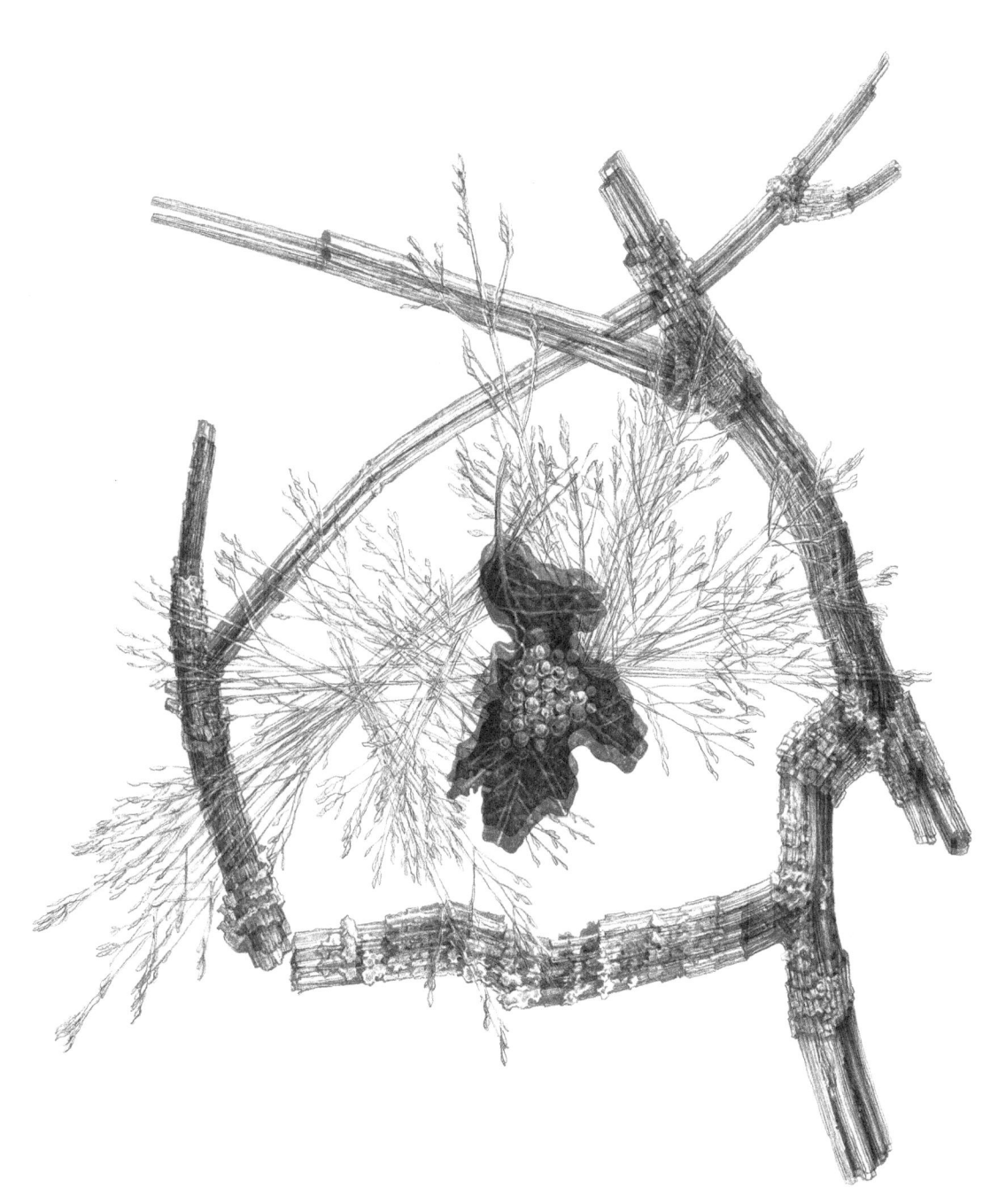

Nest

There is a little oak that lives where the river and the ocean meet. It's not very tall, reaching up perhaps as far as it reaches out. Look closer, and you will discover an intricate maze of branches, both living and dead. Twists and turns. Lines hard to follow. An outline of a life thus far. Still attached, the dead branches are completely intertwined with the living. The past and the present. Inseparable. Together. In peace.

We, the tree and I, have had many silent conversations. What we say to each other is deeper and more complex than words can describe. We have both seen struggle. We both understand loss. We both have scars. In silence, the tree shows me its life, and I reciprocate.

I see this tree as one of the most beautiful trees in the world. It shows a true representation of beauty and strength in its response to life where it finds itself. It responds honestly. Gracefully. No shame. No self-judgement. Boldly, it perseveres. Year after year, reaching up, reaching out.

It was December, a time of giving, so we blessed each other with a gift. The oak offered two little branches that fell while they were still young. I brought delicate grass from the roadside and a leaf already on the ground, shed to make space for new growth in the spring. In my other hand were beautiful, purple-blue berries from a nearby juniper tree.

I anticipated the creation of something special, but did not know exactly what it would be. I arranged the fallen branches into a circle below the tree. Then I filled the space with grass. In the middle, I carefully placed the oak leaf and filled it with berries. I realized that I, no we, had created a nest.

To me, nests are sacred circles created to gently hold something of great value. A place of protection and respect. Our nest gently held space for our unspoken conversations. A place of respect, empathy, and peace where they could rest.

There at the base of the tree, without words, we told each other we understood. Despite our hardships, we agreed to continue to reach up and reach out.

I still visit the tree where the river and the ocean meet. When I do, I tell the little tree, out loud, that I am proud of it. And at the same time, I tell myself I am proud of me, too.

As if, through our limited vision and understanding, only a tiny part of the universe, we could predict or even begin to comprehend the wonder of constant change.

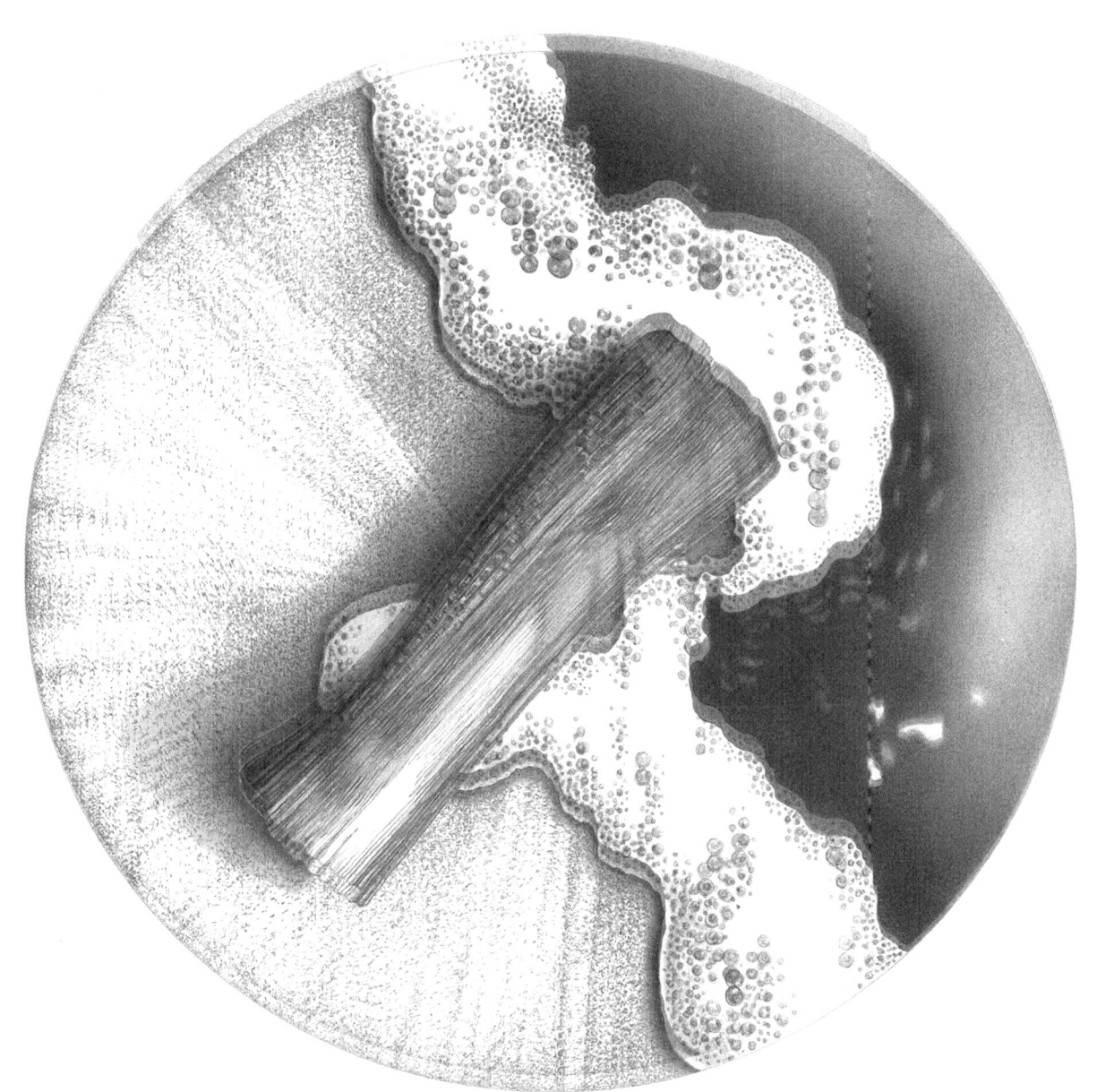

In-Between

It was the middle of winter. A time for introspection. A time for questions. A time of in-between. The landscape appeared quiet and still. But it was not. Nature is never still, constantly changing in an infinite number of ways. And yet, oblivious to the rhythm and cycles of nature, we often find ourselves surprised when things change in a way we did not anticipate. As if, through our limited vision and understanding, only a tiny part of the immense universe, we could predict or even begin to comprehend the wonder of constant change.

On that particular day, I felt a heaviness acknowledging my own in-betweenness. I went to the beach to contemplate. To hope. To look for wisdom and comfort because my life had changed. It had not turned out the way I had expected. After decades of together, I chose to be alone.

I went to a particular beach where I knew I would feel accepted. The tide was coming in and the waves slowly rolled up the long, gradual incline. I bent down low and stretched my hand towards the water. I waited. A wave came close and almost touched my hand. It receded. Another approached and then gently backed away. Slowly, respectfully, the waves came closer and closer until one lightly kissed my hand.

I stood up and glanced across the sandy expanse. I was the only person on the beach, which seemed bare of almost everything. In the distance, a single piece of wood, motionless on the sand. As I approached, I witnessed its straight, black edges. It had been cut and burned. Like me, the wood appeared to have found itself in an unexpected place. No longer a part of a tree, symbol of stability and strength, this piece of wood was now disconnected, vulnerable, and alone.

I watched as the waves approached the wood just as they had approached me. Slowly, respectfully, a little closer each time. Then, a wave touched the wood, picked it up, and carried it for a moment. "It can move!" I shouted out loud, surprising myself with my excitement. In that instant, my perspective had completely changed. Once part of a particular landscape, that piece of wood was no longer bound to the place where it began. I no longer saw it as a sad, disconnected victim of circumstance. It was in-between, positioned to start a new adventure.

As I watched, the water began to move the wood farther and farther. Part in the water, and part on land. Completely supported by water and sand, the wood could finally rest.

That day, I found the wisdom and comfort I came for. We, the wood and I, had found ourselves hurt and alone in an unexpected place. But we were in-between. No longer held to the life we once lived, we were now free to be anywhere. The "unfortunate" circumstances through which we had persevered had given us our freedom.

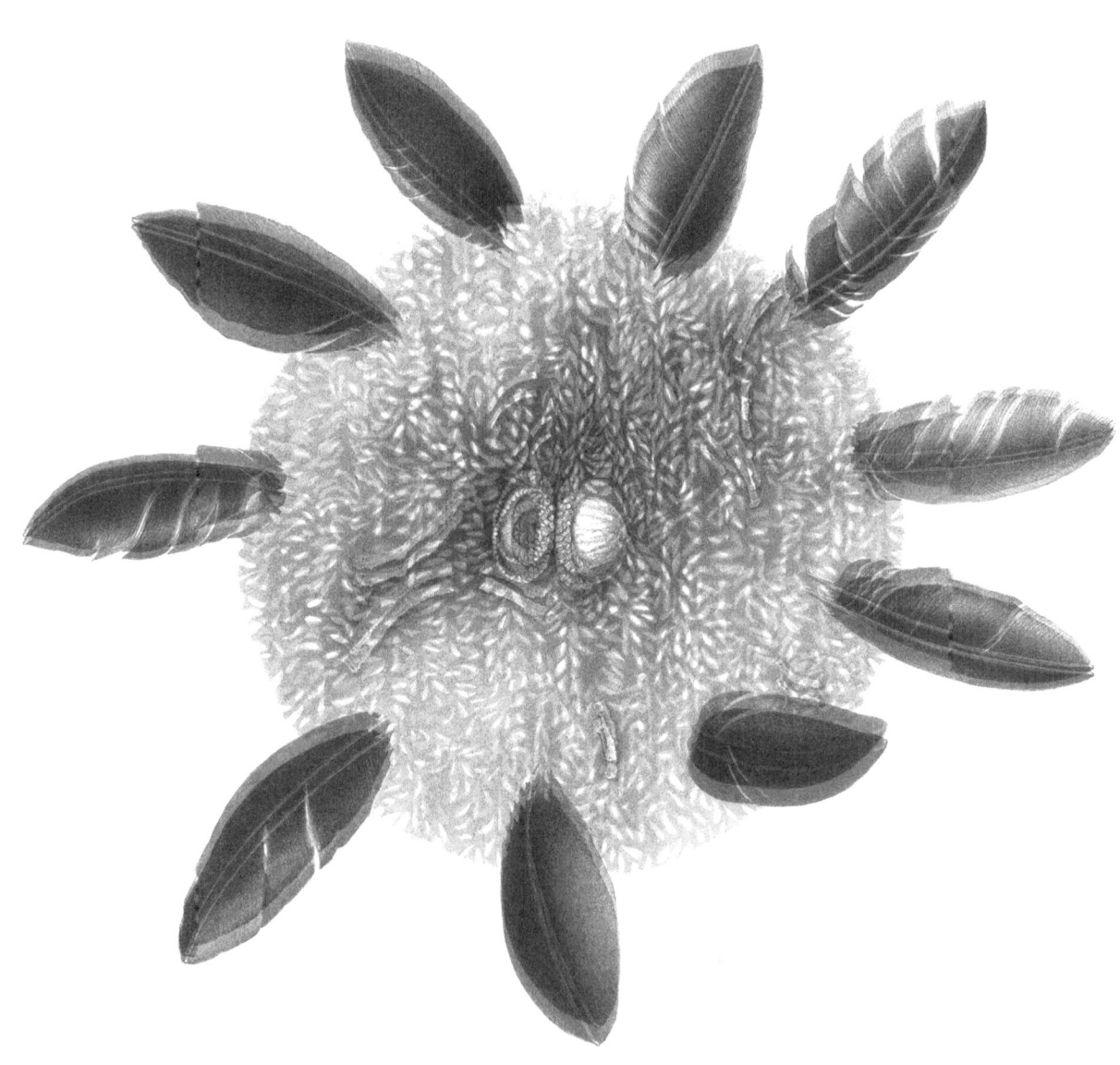

If it was my intention
to build a barrier
to protect it,
she wondered,
why would I choose to
use feathers?

Moment and Another Moment

It was my birthday and I gave myself the gift of a long walk in the woods. But it was not the peaceful walk I had hoped for. Instead, I felt unsettled, impatiently searching for something I could not find.

On that cold February day I scanned the landscape for a long time, hoping to find something to help me understand my restlessness. Finally, I saw an acorn resting on a bed of moss and decided to enclose it with a circle of crow feathers. Separate it. Make a boundary to define it. Keep it from change. It was safe now and I could rest.

A few weeks later, I told a friend about my birthday walk, the acorn, and the circle I made around it. She gently questioned my choice of feathers for the wall. If it was my intention to build a barrier to protect it, she wondered, why would I choose to use feathers? I suppose I could have enclosed it with stones, sticks, or piled dirt. Those alternatives would have been better choices for protection. But I used small crow feathers. Delicate objects made for flight. For movement. For changing direction. Perhaps my spirit held something my mind did not yet comprehend.

On that birthday walk, I believe I was looking to define myself. I wanted to say, "Here. This is who I am." I wanted to stop time and protect myself from change. But if I could do that, if I could stop time, I wouldn't experience any other moment. I would not be living. Without change, without movement, life simply ceases to be. To say, "Here is my life. This is me," would be foolish, denying the beautiful reality of change.

Over the next year, I visited the little circle often. In time, the acorn was displaced, feathers became worn, and some went missing. In the spring, new life arrived. Feather-shaped leaves appeared in the center, grew up, and bore tiny, white flowers. Two days before my next birthday, just three worn feathers remained.

Then, on my birthday, one year after making the circle of feathers, I took another walk in the same woods. This time I didn't have that unsettled, restless feeling that I did a year before. I walked along the path slowly, patiently, open to whatever I might find. This time, I wasn't looking to create something. I was looking for things to appear. I wasn't looking for a way to stop time. I was enjoying the evidence of its passing.

I approached the secret place in the woods where I had made the circle of feathers. A year after making the birthday circle, the feathers were finally gone. The delicate objects made for flight and change in direction, like the self of a year ago, had disappeared. And with them flew my restless, impatient self.

To say,
"Here is my life.
This is me,"
would be foolish,
denying the beautiful
reality of change.

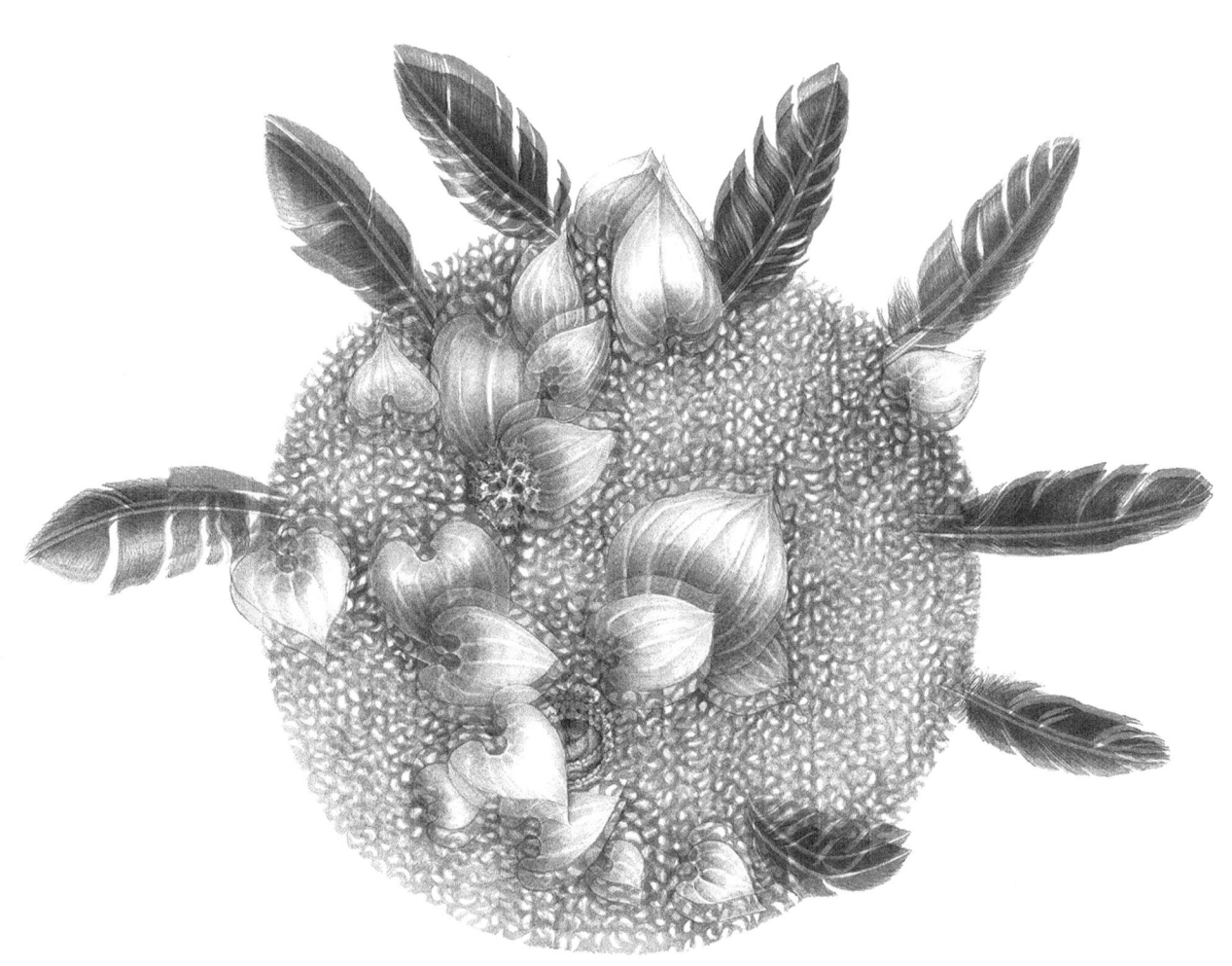

I am given the gift of holding a tiny piece of eternity. But I cannot grasp it with fingers closed. I have to open my hand to understand it.

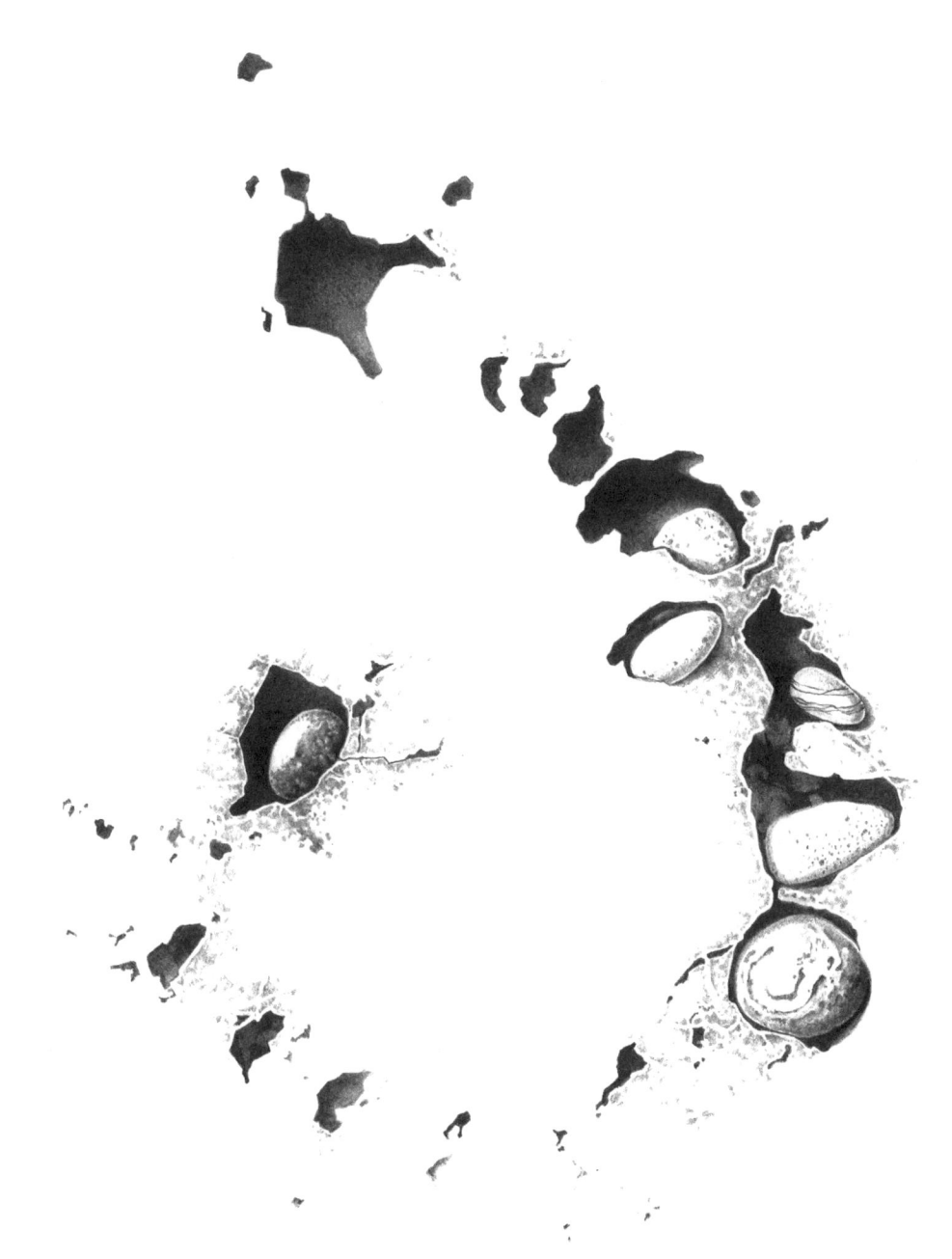

Pieces of Eternity

If you search my house right now, if you put your hands in my coat pockets, if you look on the floor of my car or beside my bed, you will find them. Rocks. They are a part of my life. I see them. I pick them up. And for a time I carry them with me as if they are mine.

I don't think I am alone in my unconscious need to interact with these ancient ones. Place a person young or old, by a rock, and they will most likely pick it up. Some will feel the need to throw it. Hurl it into a field. Skip it across a pond. Fling it hard into the ocean towards an unknown land. Others will quickly steal it away in their pocket as if they have just found something rare. That is what I do. I keep it close. On my frequent walks along the Atlantic coast, I pick often pick up a rock and roll it around on my pant leg to clean off the sand. Then I close my fingers, put my hand in my pocket, and hold the treasure tightly as I walk.

Then there are the big rocks. The wondrous layers of the Grand Canyon. The beautiful lines of red rock standing silent towards the sunset in the North American West. And massive glacial outcroppings that seem to invite us to lay down upon them and become part of the earth itself.

In New England, we have erratics along the shoreline. Like the huge rock I named "Brave One" that boldly stands alone, much farther into the ocean than all the others. Worn beautifully smooth, with the exceptional quartz vein protruding slightly above the surface, these rocks have holes and divets, made by the relentless ocean waves and spray. Sometimes I fit little rocks into the holes. Or, standing at the edge of a huge ledge, I throw small rocks back into the waves, believing that they will again find their way onto the shore, and back into my pocket once more.

I have been holding rocks for many, many years, but after all this time, I recently discovered something new. When I hold a rock with closed fingers, I feel its shape, texture, and temperature. That is about it. But if I open my palm and let the rock simply rest in my hand, I have a completely different experience. I feel its weight. Its gravity. Its wisdom. I sense agelessness. When I hold a rock in my hand, I am given the gift of holding a tiny piece of eternity. But I cannot grasp it with fingers closed. I have to open my hand to understand it.

Like the huge stone outcroppings, eternity is far too vast, too heavy, and too massive to comprehend. So the Creator, with much grace and compassion, made massive stones in such a way that they slowly and gently yield to the elements, producing smaller rocks that we may hold. Tiny stone gifts that invite us to mysteriously connect with the whole, the ageless, the eternal.

To live by the time of a bee clock, approaching moments without expectations, realizing that time can go forwards and backwards . . . sometimes at the same time.

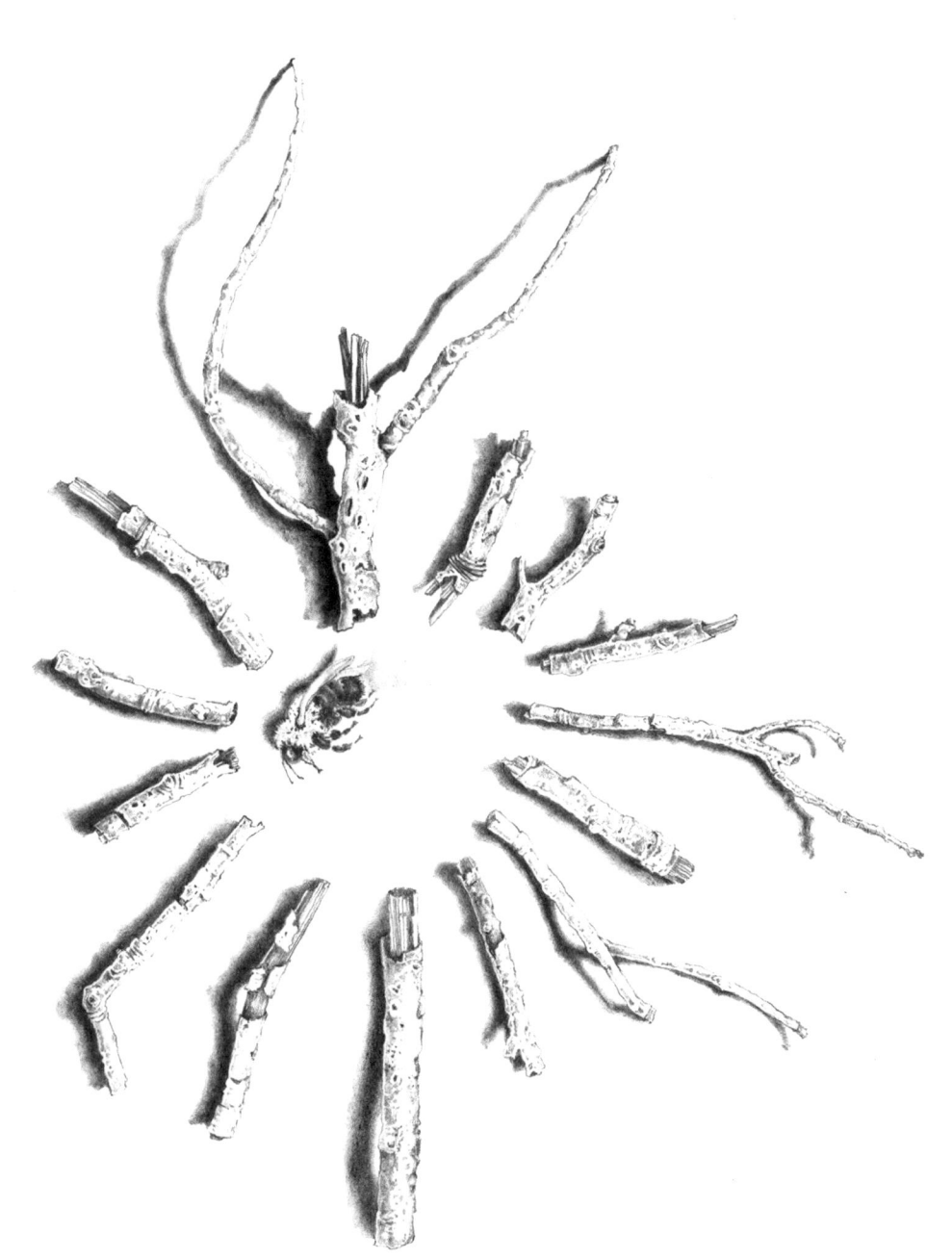

Bee Clock

In one of my favorite wooded places to walk, there is a massive, horizontal stone elevated by two man-made pedestals. It is iconic. From a distance, it looks like an altar. One day I thought it might be interesting to create a little circle on this huge, flat stone. Despite much thought, I was unsure what would be appropriate for this special place. So I decided that rather than create a circle, I would simply sit on it myself and enjoy the view.

When I approached the stone, I found the surface of the large granite slab completely bare except for one perfect little bumblebee lying still on top. A fickle spring temperature change had most likely taken his life.

Gently, I picked up the bee, placed it on another rock, and surrounded it with a circle of little beech sticks. I suppose I was trying to honor it in some way. I quietly sat with it for a while and then left.

A few weeks later, I returned to the woods and thought I would go back to the stone and see if the bee was still there. Highly unlikely, I thought, since it was such a light creature, and I had left it upon a flat rock, vulnerable to wind, rain, and visitors. To my surprise, both the bee and little beech sticks were still there. Some of the twigs had been blown about, but remained near the bee.

Quietly, I rearranged the sticks, and sat beside the reconstructed circle. What happened next can only be described as wondrous! The bee began to move! Slowly, a little at a time, the wind was moving the little creature in a perfect, counterclockwise direction within the circle of sticks. It reminded me of a clock of sorts. A clock with sticks instead of numbers. Fourteen of them. And on this clock face, the bee moved backwards instead of forwards. I began to wonder how nature would create a clock. In the natural world, time is not measured in hours or minutes. It moves in moments, cycles, and seasons. Growth. Change. Milestone moments. It is not linear. It is often unpredictable and unexpected. It can appear to pass quickly, or slowly. Sometimes time goes forwards. Sometimes it goes backwards. It can even seem to go both ways at the same time.

Everything about the bee clock was a surprise. Finding it, finding it again, and watching it move. It was an invitation to consider the pace and direction of time in nature. To live by the time of a bee clock, approaching moments without expectations, and realizing that time can go forwards and backwards... sometimes at the same time.

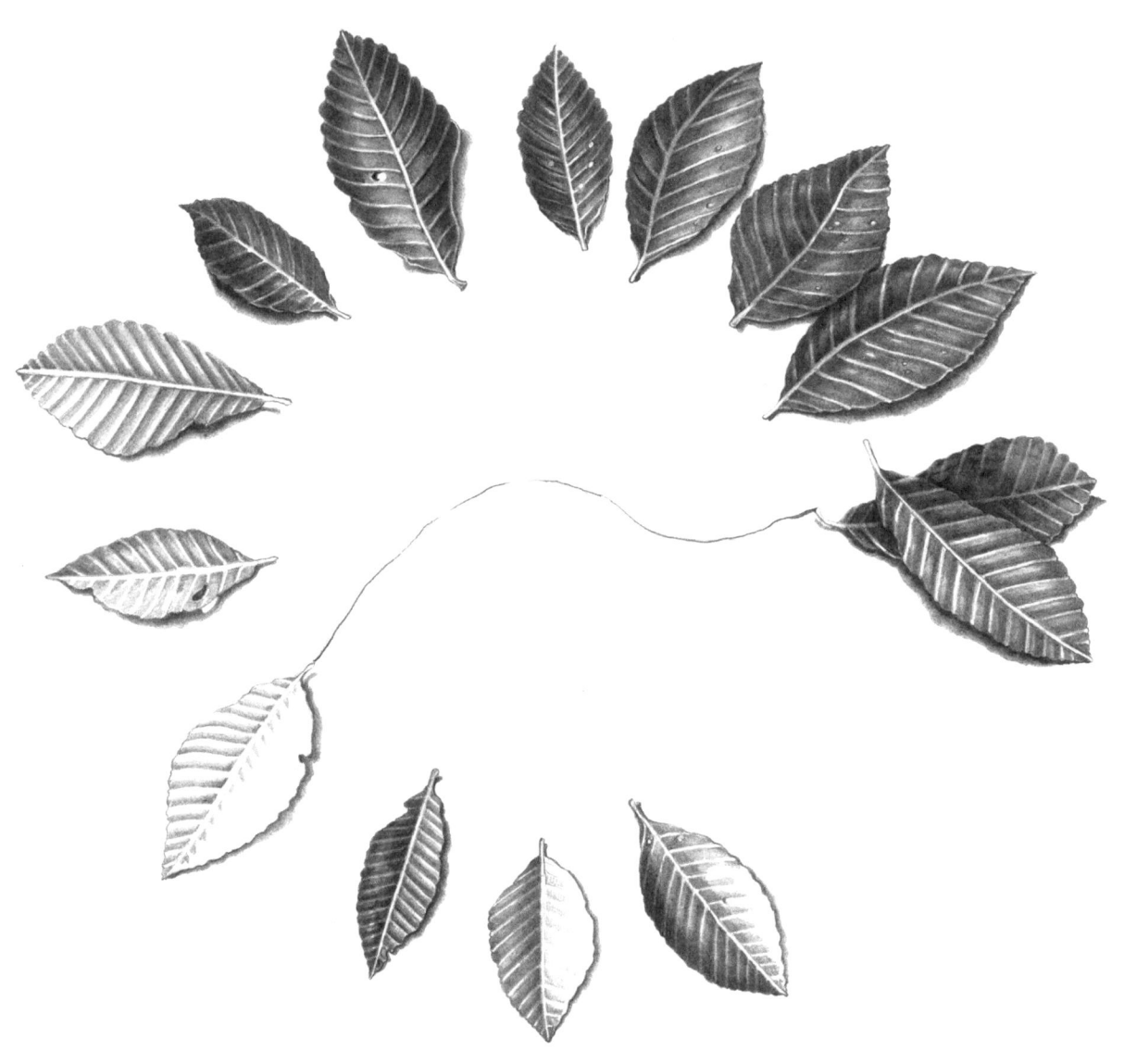

Each time it appeared,
I opened my hand
in gratitude,
and reminded myself of
the beauty of simply
being open to
everything around me.

A Spider's Gift

In an exercise in being still and observing nature's movements one day, I caught sight of an erratic, flickering light several hundred yards away. It appeared almost electric, flickering dramatically in the otherwise relatively calm woods. I walked over to investigate. I found that a spider had stretched a single line between two beech trees, and the silk was catching the light as it moved gently in the wind.

There was something special about this almost invisible string, and in an effort to immerse myself even more into the moment through observation and experience, I decided to try to imitate the movement and energy of the thin line. I must have looked absurd as I twitched in the woods, unsuccessfully imitating the flickering light. It was ridiculous. I wasn't getting it at all.

Unwilling to give up, I thought about the spider's string more intently. First, I thought, I needed to be horizontal like the thread anchored between the trees. So I lay down on a large, flat rock and waited until I felt quiet. Then came the epiphany. I realized that the spider's string was doing absolutely nothing on its own. It was the wind that was gently moving it up and down, allowing it to reflect the diffused sunlight that danced among the leaves.

As I lay on the rock, I realized my breath was making my own body gently move up and down. My breath was the wind. If I could have seen myself from a distance, I would have witnessed the slight movement in my body subtly catching the sunlight. I, like the spider's string, was not asked to do anything other than to be open to everything around me.

A few days later while driving down the road, I noticed a spider had strung a long silk thread horizontally across the entire front window inside my car. It may actually have been created on the same day I witnessed the spider's string in the woods. Very delicate, almost invisible, but strong enough to withstand the wind from my car's open windows, it become my companion for almost a year. As we traveled together, its appearance would come and go, moving in the wind and catching the dancing light through the moving landscape. Each time it appeared, I opened my hand in gratitude, and reminded myself of the beauty of simply being open to everything around me.

True prayer . . .
is the search for,
and the finding of,
some unspoken language
in which to acknowledge,
"I am here and You
are here."

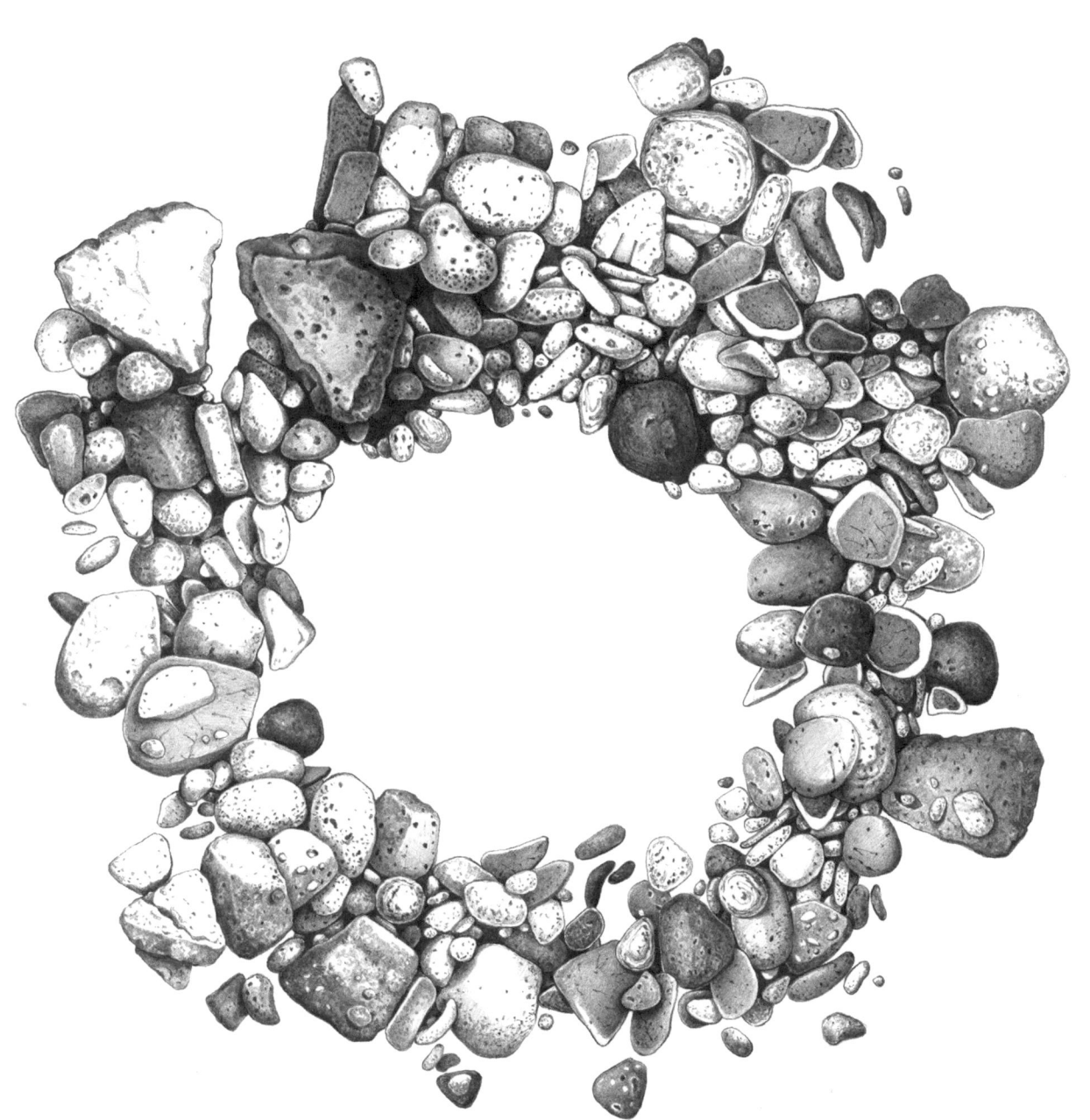

A Prayer Without Words

A prayer without words is still a prayer. Perhaps it is the purest prayer. True prayer, it seems to me, is communication between spirit and Spirit. Open. Honest. Unedited. It is the search for, and the finding of, some unspoken language in which to acknowledge, "I am here and You are here."

On one particular day, and probably for a long time without realizing it, I wanted to pray without words. I wanted to pray without the struggle for words, without hesitation, and without expectations. So I decided to create a circle, a prayer circle, my very first.

On the way out of the house, I grabbed a bag that had been sitting by the door for quite some time, the contents of which had no intended purpose. It was full of little beach bricks I had collected along the shore over a period of probably more than two decades. These pieces of man-made stone had somehow ended up in the ocean where they were broken, worn, and reshaped by time and nature. Some were collected with the kids when they were young as we searched the beach for hidden treasure. Some were from solitary walks, desperately hoping the ocean roar would block out the persistent worries in my mind. And some were from intermittent, peaceful walks.

Alone in the woods, I arranged the little pieces into a circle. I experimented placing objects in the middle. I tried feathers, a smaller circle of bricks, a piece of beach coal. I took them out. They were not right. The one circle of bricks was enough, perfect by itself. The middle needed to be empty. I enlarged the ring to where it seemed peaceful, and stopped. It was complete.

As I sat beside the little prayer circle, it became very clear to me that I had created a self-portrait. The bricks represented the physical part of my life, that which can be seen. All the plans and expectations reshaped by time and struggle, resulting in a broken and unexpected life. They represented my physical body that fought hard, held pain, but endured. I had never seen myself in this way, an accumulation of so many pieces. Now I saw the brokenness and, for the first time in my life, felt compassion for the physical me. I was no longer judgemental or impatient. I had found the long sought after peace with my circumstances and my body, which had to adapt to the places it found itself. In its brokenness, it was somehow beautiful. It was me.

The inside circle, the open space, represented the unseen. The mystery. The spiritual. A place deliberately left open and uncluttered where spirit and Spirit can meet.

Together, the two parts of my circle symbolize the seen and the unseen. The physical and the spiritual. A personal and also universal self-portrait. Within my wordless prayer, I had created a sacred place where I could say, without words, "I am here and You are here."

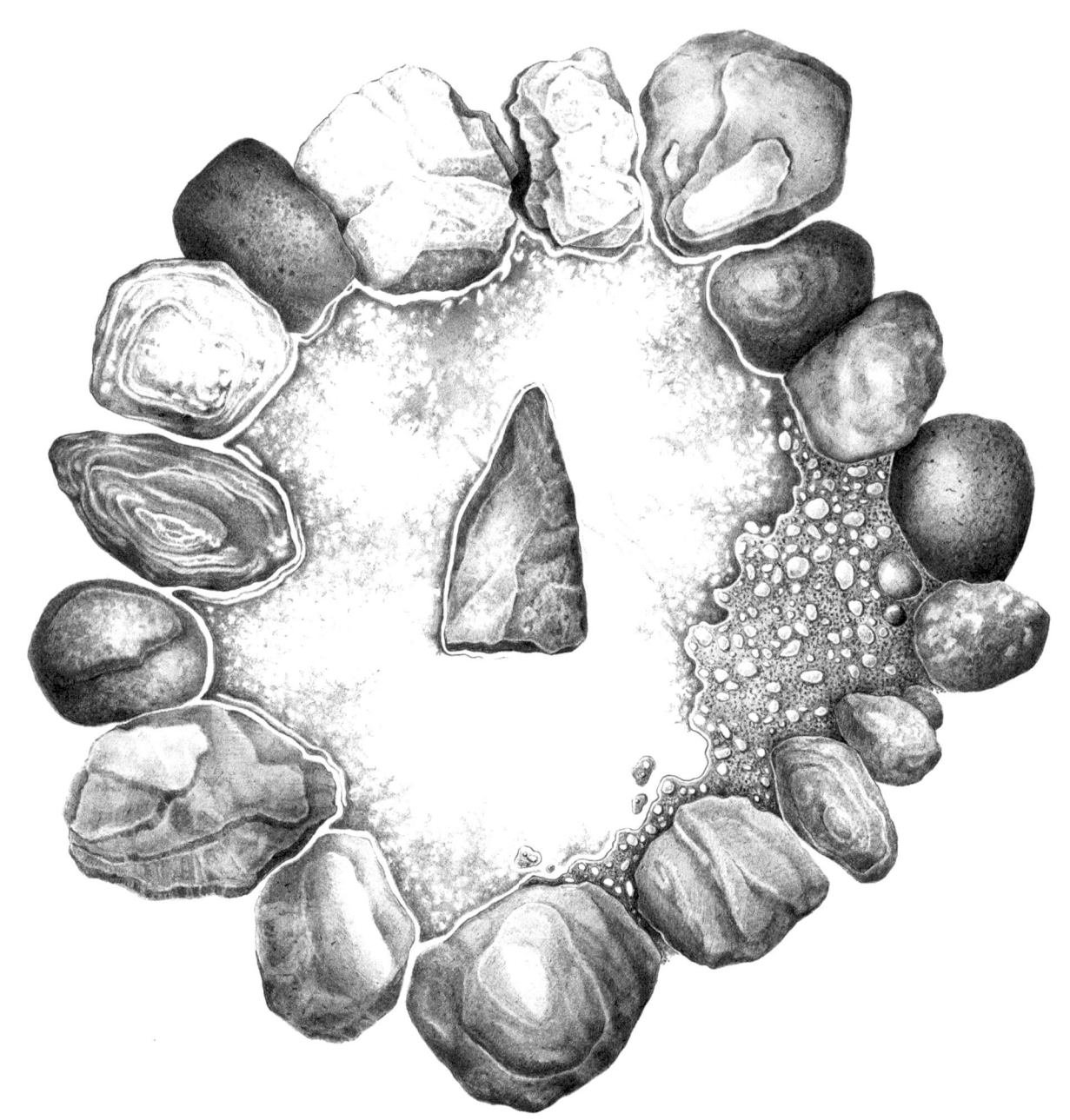

And the riverbed replied,

"Patience."

Walking in a Dry Riverbed

Impatience. That was my word as I walked in a dry riverbed for several weeks that summer. "There should be water. There should be life. There should be flow. There should be direction," I would think to myself while walking on the newfound path where one of my favorite streams usually ran. But it was dry. No water. No direction. No flow. And the riverbed replied, "Patience."

I walked upstream looking for its source, as if I could find it. As if I could see what the trouble was. I don't think I had ever seen this stream completely dry. But there wasn't any trouble. It had been a hot summer and the riverbed was dry. It just was.

I gathered some rocks from the streambed and made a circle on the dry earth where the water usually flows. In the middle I placed a triangular stone pointing downstream, encouraging the water to return and reminding it of its path.

Over the next several weeks, I regularly checked the weather report, intently watching for rain. After each summer shower, I anxiously returned to the water's path, expecting a deluge. But still, no water. Several more trips. Nothing.

It takes a long time to fill up a dry riverbed. It takes more than one brief rain. It requires steady rainfall or storms when it is that dry. Like many things in nature, many things in life, restoration takes time.

After several rains, I discovered a little water had collected inside my circle. Days of steady rain followed and the circle gradually covered over.

One of the most interesting things I have learned in my first year of circles was that my mind and my spirit often see things from two completely different perspectives. My mind says, "Hey!" and is impatient with the water. But my spirit says, "Wait," and instinctively knows that things will change. In difficult times, I remind myself, "Don't be so hard on yourself. Don't be so impatient. It is just a season." To encourage myself I say, "It will come. It just takes time."

My little circle of river rocks is still there. I visit it often. Sometimes, I cannot see the circle because of the water's depth, reflections, or debris temporarily caught up in the stones. But I know it is there. It is a silent witness and reminder of the seasons of dryness and flow. Impatience and patience.

If the riverbed becomes dry again next year, I will walk it and repair my little circle of rocks. I will see what else I can learn as I walk more slowly, more patiently, knowing that there will be life, there will be flow, there will be direction once again.

Hope is a dream
inside a prayer.
It is a patient little
message from the heart,
thrown freely
out into the world.

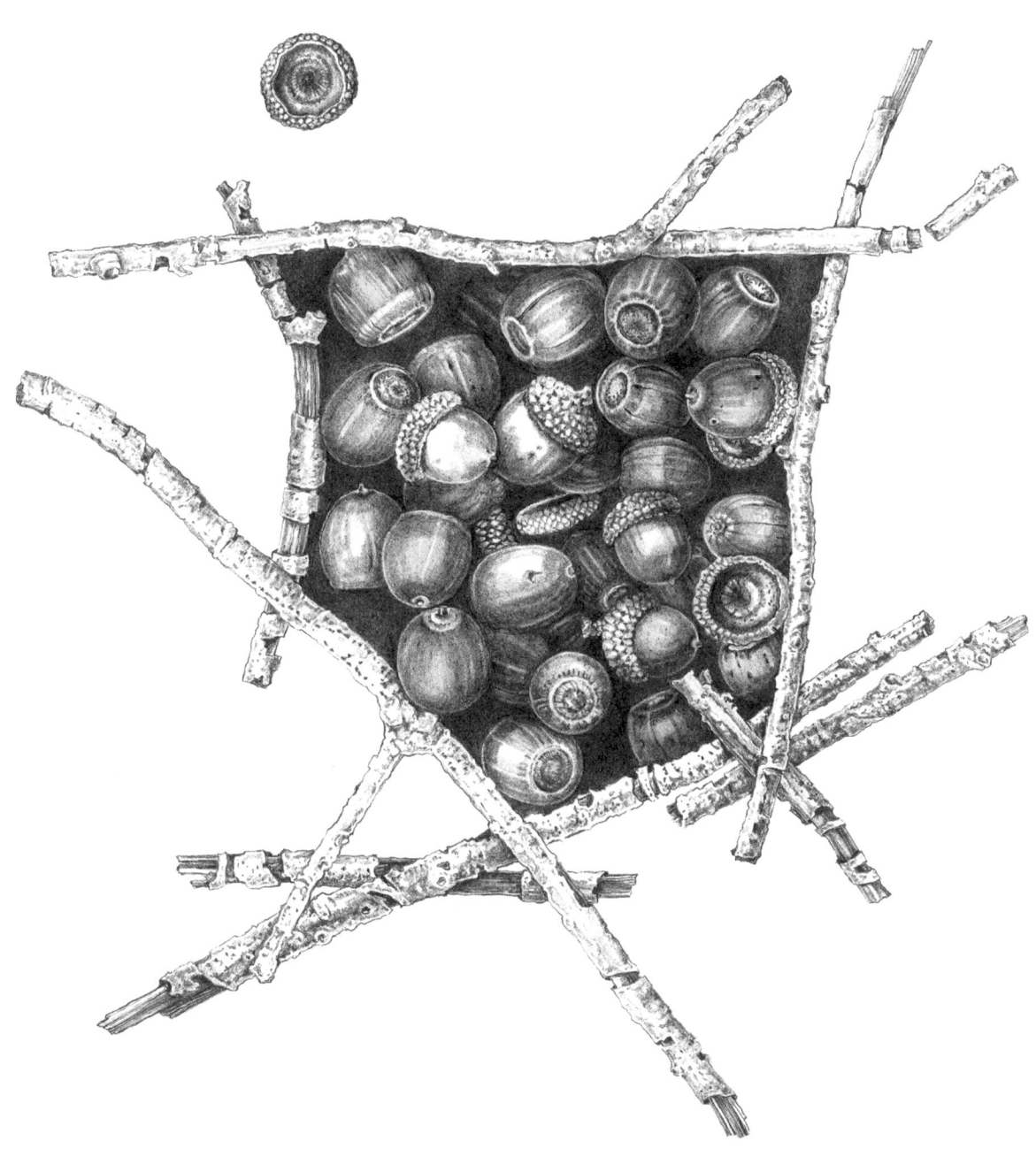

Gathering Hopes

When I was a young girl, someone told me he didn't like fall: "It is like death," he said. Despite this dark introduction to the season, fall has become one of my favorite times of the year. To me, it is not about death. It is all about the beginning of new life!

Every year, I get excited about the promise of a new year and usually start thinking about it long before the first of January. But I am not one for New Year's resolutions. I think a list of do's and don'ts is life draining. To me, identifying hopes and dreams is far more encouraging and exciting. So, yes, I think about the new year in the fall. Because a new year doesn't necessarily start in January. It starts when you define and plant your hopes.

As I walked by myself in the woods one autumn day, I found evidence that another person had been enjoying the same path in what seemed to be a mast year for acorns. They had made three piles on a large, flat rock. One was a group of little fallen branches. The second, a mound of very short, fat sticks. The third was a gathering of acorns. I loosened the pile of branches, opening up a space in the middle. Then I gathered some of the acorns and placed them in the center. It looked beautiful to me and I hoped the acorn collector would agree.

As I continued to walk under holly, beech, and oak, the acorns continued to fall, hard, all over the place. "A million acorns! A million possibilities! A million hopes for the spring!" I silently cheered with childlike enthusiasm as I witnessed acorns raining from the sky. I decided that when I returned home, I would list a million hopes for the coming year. I would write quickly, from the heart, letting whatever came to mind make it onto the list.

And so I did: I listed my hopes. In the end, I didn't have a million, but I did have sixty, and sixty hopes is a wonderful thing! Straight from the heart. Written just as they came. My eclectic list. Some of my hopes were, "I will make it through the winter. I will lay down on some great, red rocks out West. I will listen to the wind more. I will live by turkeys." I love my list!

This year, with the help of a million acorns, I created my own definition of hope. Hope is a dream inside a prayer. It is a patient little message from the heart, thrown freely out into the world.

There are forces with whom we are deeply connected but do not understand and cannot control. I think our hopes somehow connect to that unknown. They are like acorns. When they are ready, they let go, they are gathered, and then they rest.

And sometimes they grow.

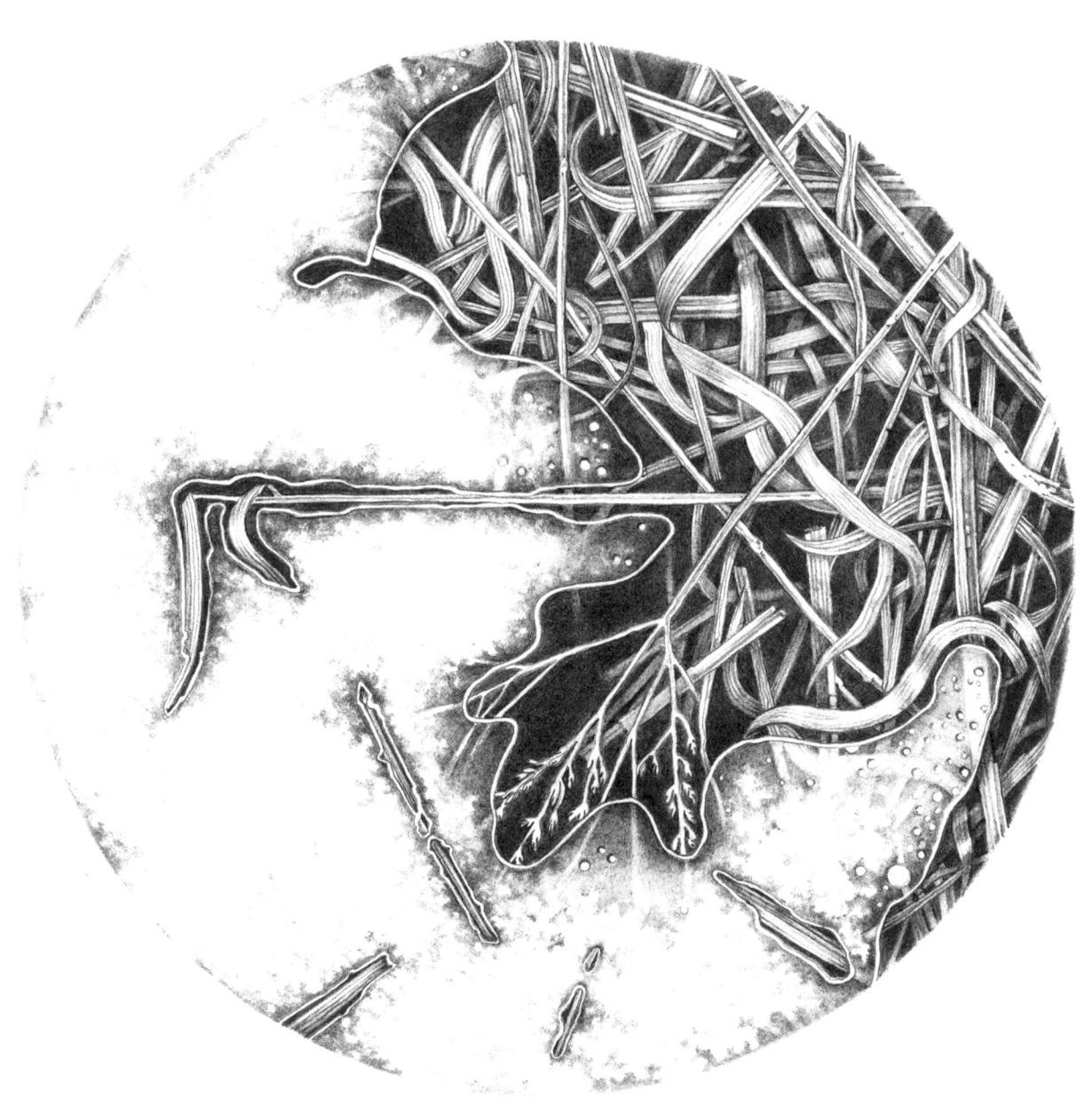

It is winter.
The cornfield is frozen.
The plants of Before have died, but the seeds of Next have not yet stirred. It is a place called Wait.

A Place Called Wait

There is a place called Wait. It is hard to find, and it takes a long, long time to get there. There are many paths to this place of no location, as many paths as there are travelers. Each path and journey is different and can only be traveled by one. No one can lead and no one can follow. The path is always, and only, just for one.

In this place called Wait, there are no emotions. The traveler has lost them. Shed them. Discarded them. Gradually left them in little pieces along the path until completely gone. Wait is past fear. It is beyond hope. It has no expectations. It doesn't ponder. It only, only waits.

The journey to this place involves struggle in some form. It may be short or long, but is usually long. You will, however, know when you have arrived because you cannot take another step. Looking back, you see that every footprint has disappeared.

You have arrived. Now you stand. Stand alone. Wait. If you are fortunate, however, you realize that Wait can be a place of rest and freedom. You are required to do nothing but : : : wait.

Not all people complete this long and arduous journey. There are many distractions along the way. It is a lonely, sometimes scary place, only for the strong. But those who complete the journey eventually find themselves in a good place because Wait is the gateway to Allow, which eventually leads to Finally. And Finally is a sweet, sweet place.

It is winter. The cornfield is frozen. The plants of Before have died, and the seeds of Next are not yet awake. It is a place called Wait.

Then a bird sings. The wind changes direction. And the ground moves. The field is green again!

Finally.

But as interesting as the
intricate lines and details of
the old wood were,
it was the empty part,
the part where the stump
was no longer visible,
that I went to see.

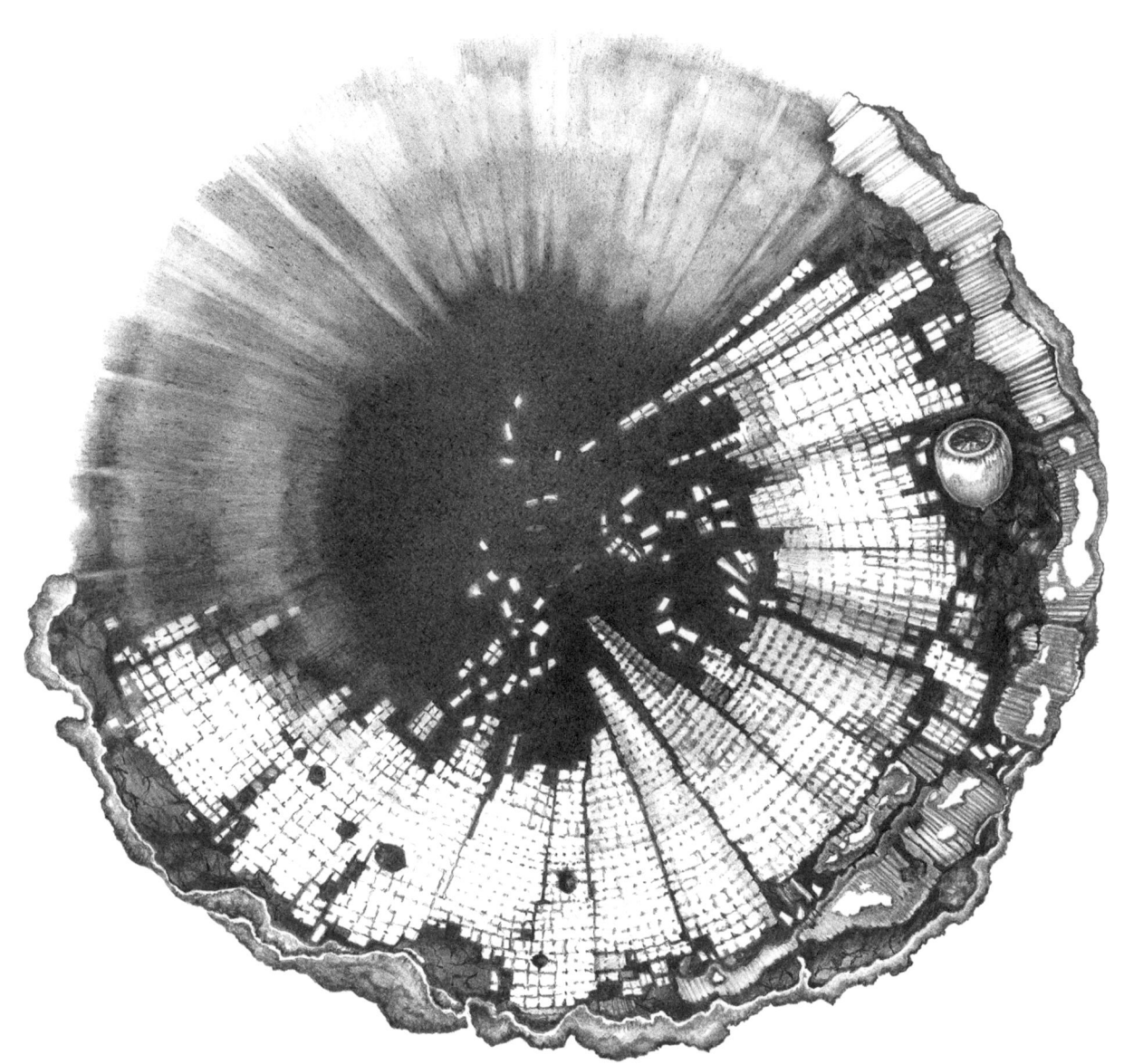

Letting Go, Gently

During this *Year of Sacred Circles*, I began to visit a particular stump in the woods. But as interesting as the intricate lines and details of the old wood were, it was the empty part, the part where the stump was no longer visible, that I went to see. Each time I walked towards it, I hoped to find something new had entered the empty space. A surprise. Usually it was a few fallen oak or beech leaves. Sometimes an acorn.

During that time, I was wrestling with two very different losses in my life, one of which made me angry. The other made me incredibly sad. Since I was drawn to the stump that had also suffered loss, I hoped it had a message for me.

I, like many, have faced significant challenges in my life and if I were to give you a chronological outline of my life so far, you might guess which things I find hard to get over. But you would probably be wrong. It is sometimes not the obvious that trips us up. It is what is deep within the heart. At some point in my life I began to say, "Life is a struggle," or "My life is all about struggle." I would say it with bitterness. Attach an emotion to the words, flinging them into the air where they seemed to change into "Hey God! Remember me?" Or "Hey God! What's up with this?"

In reality, life *is* often a struggle. But what if struggle was a beautiful thing? What if the challenges that are in our paths make us strong and beautiful?

It has taken me a very long time to recognize my character strengths. Today, I would say that in some ways I am brave, resilient, compassionate, sensitive, and open. But I would not have these qualities had it not been for the path I have walked, without the struggles I have endured. Bravery would not exist without having jumped into the unknown. Resilience could not be developed without prolonged struggle. Compassion has come from surviving indifference. Sensitivity has known pain. And openness has witnessed judgement, but chooses not to judge. These parts of me, the strengths, were born in the empty part of the stump's circle. This part of the circle that let go of what was there, in order to make room for something else. It is the part you cannot see, but that which makes the circle whole.

When I look at my life with anger and sadness over my losses, I am looking at the stump. The visible. The brokenness. But that is only part of me. That is not the whole. By gently letting go, I begin to make space for something to replace it.

It can be incredibly difficult to let go. Painful. Raw. Long. So very long. For this reason, I add the word "gently" to the letting go, and when I do, I become more compassionate and patient with myself and others.

I know it will take time. I need not rush. I will simply begin by letting go . . . gently.

the end

the beginning

www.ingramcontent.com/pod-product-compliance
Lightning Source LLC
Chambersburg PA
CBHW051923210526
45473CB00006B/2120